GL

ASK ISAAC ASIMOV

WHY DO WE NEED SLEEP?

BY ISAAC ASIMOV AND CARRIE DIERKS

Gareth Stevens Publishing
MILWAUKEE

For a free color catalog describing Gareth Stevens's list of high-quality children's books, call 1-800-341-3569 (USA) or 1-800-461-9120 (Canada).

The editor would like to thank Robert A. Rosen, M.D., of Newtowne Medical Group, Milwaukee, Wisconsin, for his invaluable assistance regarding the accuracy of the text.

Library of Congress Cataloging-in-Publication Data

Asimov, Isaac, 1920-
    Why do we need sleep? / by Isaac Asimov and Carrie Dierks.
       p. cm. -- (Ask Isaac Asimov)
    Includes bibliographical references and index.
    Summary: A brief discussion of sleep, why we need it, what happens
when we sleep, and sleep disorders.
    ISBN 0-8368-0806-1
    1. Sleep--Juvenile Literature. [1. Sleep.] I. Dierks, Carrie.
II. Title. III. Series: Asimov, Isaac, 1920-   Ask Isaac Asimov.
    RA786.A78 1993
    612.8'21--dc20   93-20154

Edited, designed, and produced by
Gareth Stevens Publishing
1555 North RiverCenter Drive, Suite 201
Milwaukee, Wisconsin 53212, USA

Picture Credits
pp. 2-3, © Horvath/Chris Fairclough Colour Library; pp. 4-5, © Horvath/Chris Fairclough Colour Library; pp. 6-7, Tom Redman, 1993; pp. 8-9, Tom Redman, 1993; pp. 10-11, © SIU/Visuals Unlimited; pp. 12-13, Tom Redman, 1993; pp. 14-15, Tom Redman, 1993; pp. 16-17, Tom Redman, 1993; pp. 18-19, Tom Redman, 1993; pp. 20-21, Tom Redman, 1993; pp. 22-23, Tom Redman, 1993; p. 24, Tom Redman, 1993

Cover photograph, © Jon Allyn, Cr. Photog., 1993: Most of the time, sleeping means sweet dreams.

Series editor: Barbara J. Behm
Series designer: Sabine Beaupré
Book designer: Kristi Ludwig
Art coordinator: Karen Knutson
Picture researcher: Diane Laska

Printed in the United States of America

1 2 3 4 5 6 7 8 9 98 97 96 95 94 93

Contents

Words that appear in the glossary are printed in **boldface** type the first time they occur in the text.

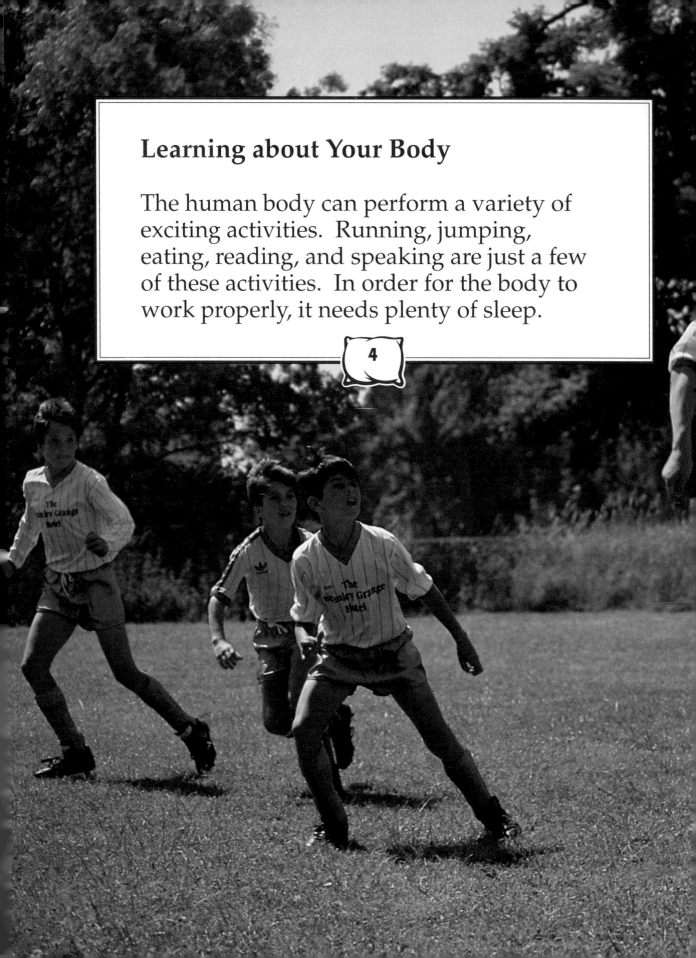

Learning about Your Body

The human body can perform a variety of exciting activities. Running, jumping, eating, reading, and speaking are just a few of these activities. In order for the body to work properly, it needs plenty of sleep.

4

What happens to our bodies and our brains while we are sleeping? What happens if we don't get enough sleep? Let's find out.

Time for Bed!

You've had a busy day — school, homework, chores, and playing with friends. Your eyelids feel heavy and start to droop. You're ready to fall asleep.

6

After turning out the lights and snuggling under the covers, you slowly begin to relax. Your eyes close, and everything in the room gets a little cloudy. As you drift off to sleep, your heartbeat and breathing rate slow down. Your body temperature also drops.

7

A Good Night's Sleep

Most young children sleep from nine to eleven hours each night. As a tiny baby, you probably slept a total of sixteen hours a day. A newborn wakes up several times throughout the day and night. By the time a baby is a year old, he or she is usually sleeping through the night and taking one or two naps during the day. As children get older, they need less and less sleep until they are fully grown. Most adults need seven or eight hours of sleep a night.

4 p.m. to 8 p.m.	8 p.m. to midnight	midnight to 4 a.m.	4 a.m. to 8 a.m.	8 a.m. to noon	noon to 4 p.m.
MOTHER: *Awake*	MOTHER: *Asleep*	MOTHER: *Awake*	MOTHER: *Asleep*	MOTHER: *Awake*	MOTHER: *Awake*
FATHER: *Awake*	FATHER: *Asleep*	FATHER: *Asleep*	FATHER: *Awake*	FATHER: *Awake*	FATHER: *Awake*
TOM: *Awake*	TOM: *Asleep*	TOM: *Asleep*	TOM: *Asleep*	TOM: *Awake*	TOM: *Awake*
BABY: *Asleep*	BABY: *Asleep*	BABY: *Awake*	BABY: *Asleep*	BABY: *Asleep*	BABY: *Awake*

The Science of Sleep

How do scientists know what happens when you sleep? They study electrical waves given off by the brain. An instrument called an **electroencephalograph** (EEG) measures **brain waves** and records them on a **graph**.

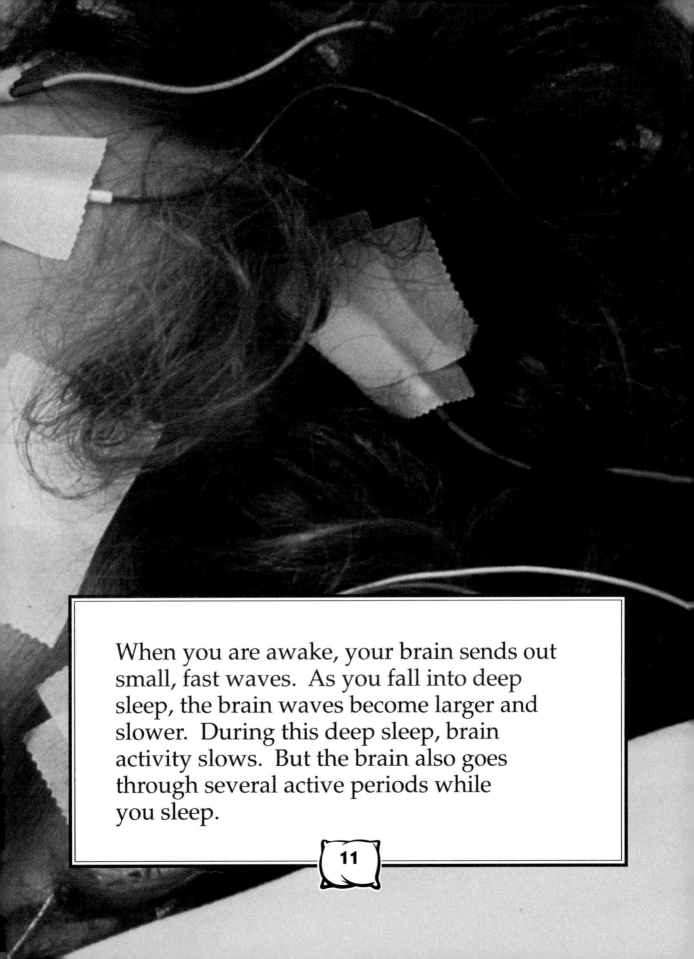

When you are awake, your brain sends out small, fast waves. As you fall into deep sleep, the brain waves become larger and slower. During this deep sleep, brain activity slows. But the brain also goes through several active periods while you sleep.

11

Your Busy Brain

Every 90 to 100 minutes during sleep, your brain begins to send out shorter, faster waves. These sleep periods are called **REM sleep**, for "rapid eye movement." If you look at a sleeping person and see that her or his eyes are moving quickly back and forth, you know the person is in REM sleep. During REM sleep, there is a greater flow of blood and oxygen to the brain and greater body movement, including twitching.

Healthy sleepers have about four REM periods per night. Each of them lasts from five to fifteen minutes. People **dream** during REM sleep.

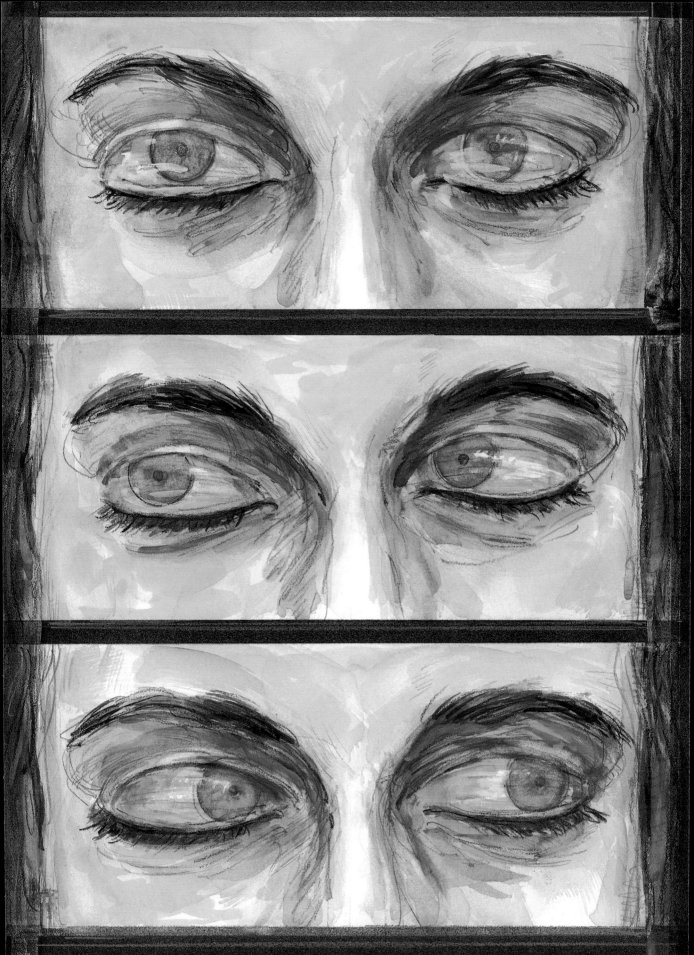

Sweet Dreams!

Everyone dreams, but do you remember your dreams? Generally, some people remember their dreams, and others don't. Dreams may seem strange and unnatural, or they may be very true to life. But dreams are usually related to a person's experiences. Many people believe that studying dreams helps them understand their innermost thoughts and feelings.

You're Getting Sleepy . . .

Scientists don't know exactly how sleep refreshes us. But they do know that we can't get along without sleep. If you have ever missed a good night's sleep, you probably felt tired and ill the next day. Perhaps you also had trouble concentrating.

16

People who have not slept for several days have even more trouble. They must stay active all the time to keep from dozing off. They can't think clearly and may even imagine they see things that are not there.

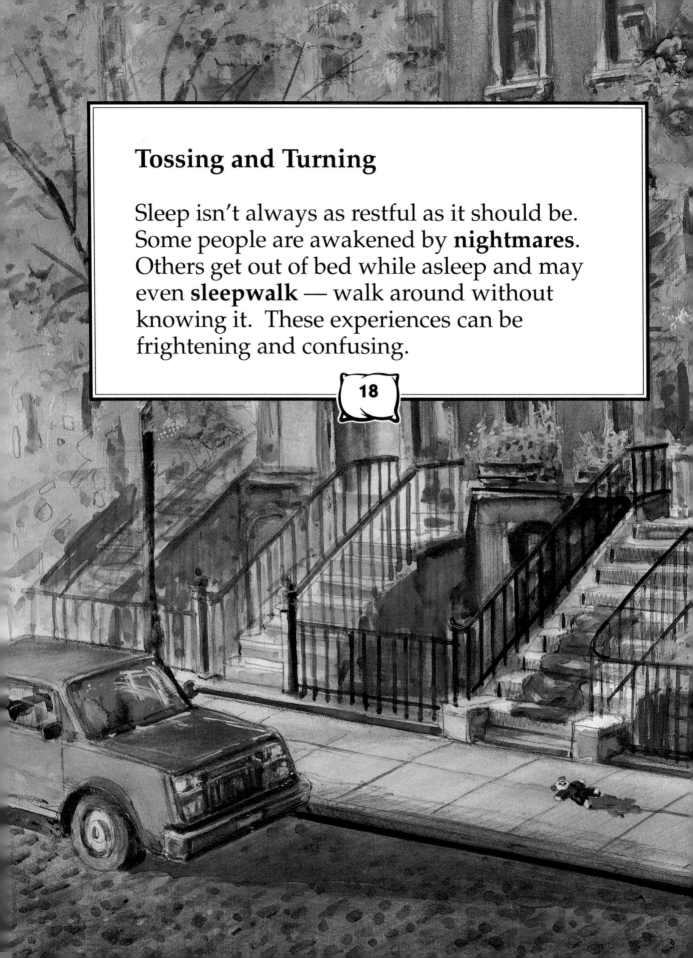

Tossing and Turning

Sleep isn't always as restful as it should be. Some people are awakened by **nightmares**. Others get out of bed while asleep and may even **sleepwalk** — walk around without knowing it. These experiences can be frightening and confusing.

18

Other people have great trouble falling asleep — a condition called **insomnia**. Imagining a pleasant scene and even counting sheep might help a person fall asleep. But people with severe insomnia may need a doctor's care.

19

Animal Slumber

Other animals, besides humans, need their rest, too. Some, like fish and insects, don't actually sleep. They just slow down and rest for a while each day. Other animals, such as bears, spend the entire winter in a deep sleep called **hibernation**. During hibernation, the heartbeat and breathing rate slow down, and body temperature drops. For nutrition, the animal lives off of stored body fat.

Do animals dream? Yes! EEGs show that animals go through REM sleep, just like humans do. But we can only guess what animals might be dreaming.

The Mysteries of Sleep

Humans spend about one-third of their lives sleeping. Yet there are many unanswered questions about sleep. Why do humans need sleep, while many other animals only need rest? Why are some people "early birds," while others are "night owls?" What do dreams really mean? As scientists learn more about the brain, perhaps they will solve these mysteries of sleep.

22

More Books to Read

The Seven Sleepers: The Story of Hibernation by Phyllis S. Busch
    (Macmillan)
Sleep and Dreams by Alvin Silverstein and Virginia B. Silverstein
    (Harper & Row Junior)
Sleep and Its Disorders in Children by Christian Guilleminault
    (Raven)
Sleep: Our Unknown Life by Richard Deming (Thomas Nelson, Inc.)
Sleeping and Dreaming by R. Milios (Childrens Press)
What Happens When You Sleep? by Joy Richardson (Gareth Stevens)

Places to Write

Here are some places you can write for more information about
sleep. Be sure to tell them exactly what you want to know. Give
them your full name and address so they can write back to you.

American Sleep Disorders Association
1610 14th Street N.W., Suite 300
Rochester, MN 55901

Association for the Study of Dreams
P.O. Box 1600
Vienna, VA 22183

Canadian Sleep Society
Department of Psychology
Queens University
Kingston, Ontario
K7G 3N6

Glossary

brain waves: rhythmic changes between parts of the brain.

dream: to have various thoughts, images, and emotions during sleep.

electroencephalograph (ee-LECK-tro-en-SEF-el-oh-graff): an instrument that traces and records brain waves.

graph (grăff): a diagram that plots the changes in something.

hibernation (hye-berr-NA-shun): a state of rest or inactivity.

insomnia (in-SOM-nee-ah): a state of being unable to sleep for an extended period of time.

nightmare: a frightening dream.

REM sleep: the period of sleep where the eyes move quickly back and forth.

sleepwalk: to walk while asleep without being aware of it.

Index